BRILLIANT WOMEN

AMAZING ARTISTS AND DESIGNERS

Written by Georgia Amson-Bradshaw
Illustrated by Rita Petruccioli

BARRON'S

D1401289

CONTENTS

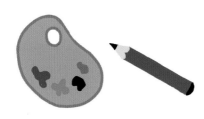

AMAZING ARTISTS AND DESIGNERS

What's the most famous painting you can think of? Probably the *Mona Lisa*, right? Many of the most famous paintings in the world are of beautiful women. Pictures like Leonardo da Vinci's portrait of Mona Lisa or Sandro Botticelli's *The Birth of Venus* are instantly recognizable works of art, famous the world over.

But although galleries and art museums might be full of pictures of women, when it comes to pictures made by women, it's a different story. Only between three and five percent of the artworks on display in the most famous galleries across Europe and the USA are by women artists.

Despite not always being given prominence in museum and gallery collections, women have been making incredible art for hundreds of years. The styles of art might be very different, ranging from Artemisia Gentileschi's baroque painting to Louise Bourgeois' huge, twisted metal sculptures and Lee Miller's surrealist photography, but they are united by their talent and dedication to their art.

Some of the women in this book were well-known in their lifetime, some of them were not. Some are still working to break the boundaries of art as we know it today, but all of them are amazingly gifted and talented women, who created important art, design, fashion, and architecture.

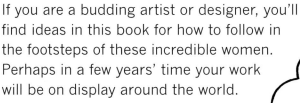

If you are a budding artist or designer, you'll find ideas in this book for how to follow in the footsteps of these incredible women. Perhaps in a few years' time your work will be on display around the world.

So read on, and be inspired by these brilliant women's stories.

Take a look at **pages 44–45** to find out how YOU can get involved in art and design.

ARTEMISIA GENTILESCHI

An incredibly talented painter, Artemisia Gentileschi created scenes full of passion and drama.

BAROQUE

Artemisia was an artist in the baroque style, which typically shows scenes from the Bible painted in an atmospheric, dramatic, and detailed way.

LIVED: July 8, 1593–c. 1656

BORN IN: Rome (Italy)

WORKED IN: Italy and England

Artemisia was born in Rome, Italy in 1593. She was the eldest child of the painter Orazio Gentileschi. Although there were many famous painters and sculptors in Italy around that time, women were not normally allowed to train as artists. But Orazio saw that Artemesia was much more talented than her brothers, and realized it was worth teaching her. Despite becoming a very accomplished painter, unlike other artists of the time, she was never taught to read or write!

In her dad's studio Artemesia learned to draw, to mix pigments, and how to paint in the chiaroscuro style. Chiaroscuro is a technique that was popularized by the famous artist Caravaggio, who was a friend of Orazio Gentileschi. It uses areas of strong light and shade to create very dramatic scenes. Artemisia excelled in this style.

When she was only 17, Artemesia painted a scene from the Bible, *Susanna and the Elders*. It shows two old men spying on Susanna as she bathes. Unlike other versions of the scene from the same era, Artemisia's version of the story shows Susanna's emotion and suffering. Her eyes are full of tears, and her body is twisted in embarrassment.

Artemisia moved to Florence in 1614 and became very successful. She was commissioned to produce artworks for the rich and powerful Medici family, as well as King Charles I of Great Britain. She became the first woman to be allowed to join the Accademia della Arti del Disegno (the Academy of the Arts and Design) and became friends with other influential people, including the scientist Galileo Galilei.

Throughout her career she painted many images of strong and defiant women. One of her most famous paintings is called *Judith Slaying Holofernes*, which is a gory picture of the beautiful widow Judith, killing Holofernes, an army general who was about to destroy her city. During her lifetime Artemisia's work was very well known and admired. A portrait of her painted by another artist at the time describes her as "the famous Roman painter."

After her death Artemisia was mostly forgotten by art critics, and many of her paintings were assumed to be done by male artists. In the 20th century, art historians began to reassess her importance as an artistic figure. Through painstakingly examining artworks from the period, historians have been able to identify from tiny details, such as types of brushstroke, which paintings were in fact created by Artemisia. She is now considered one of the most talented painters of her generation.

PAINT LIKE ARTEMISIA

Create your own chiaroscuro artwork. Set up a still-life scene that you would like to draw or paint, perhaps a selection of fruit, or an ornament, or a figurine. Draw the curtains or dim the light, so the room is dark, and place a flashlight or lamp so that it shines light on your still-life scene from an angle. Sketch the object or objects, trying to capture how the light falls on one side, while the other side is in shade.

ROSA BONHEUR

An animal lover with a strong independent streak, Rosa Bonheur painted horses, bulls, and other animals in a naturalistic style.

ANIMALIER

Rosa Bonheur was known as an animalier, an artist skilled in the realistic portrayal of animals.

LIVED:	March 16, 1822–May 25, 1899
BORN IN:	Bordeaux (France)
WORKED IN:	France, Scotland, and England

Rosa always loved animals. What Rosa did NOT love was school. Even as a very young child she would sit happily sketching animals for hours on end, but when her mom tried to teach her to read and write, Rosa would stubbornly refuse. Eventually her mom came up with the idea of getting Rosa to draw an animal for each letter of the alphabet, and she learned her letters that way!

Rosa was the eldest child in a family of artists. Her family belonged to a Christian sect called the Saint-Simonians who, unusually for the time, believed in the equal education of women. But formal education did not suit Rosa. She was a very naughty pupil and was expelled from many different schools due to her disruptive behavior. After being expelled from another school when she was 12, her father decided to teach Rosa to be a painter.

EXPELLED

10

Rosa began by copying pictures of animals from books, before moving on to making studies of live animals. She would travel to the outskirts of Paris to paint the horses, sheep, cows, and goats there. Her most famous painting is *The Horse Fair*, a huge artwork that measures 8 ft (2.5 m) tall and 16 ft (5 m) wide. It shows the horse market in Paris, and is now on display in the Metropolitan Museum in New York, USA.

When Rosa's work was displayed in Britain it caught the attention of the art critics and collectors there, and she met Queen Victoria who admired her paintings. Her rise in popularity abroad was not matched at home because French art critics began to consider her style "too English." They started referring to her with the English title "Miss" rather than "Mademoiselle."

In spite of the criticism from her fellow countrymen, Rosa became very famous in Britain and the USA. During the 1860s American girls could own Rosa Bonheur dolls, and engravings of her painting *The Horse Fair* were given away with American newspapers as a free gift.

Rosa did things differently throughout her whole life. She had a fifty-year relationship with her partner, artist Nathalie Micas, at a time when gay relationships were considered scandalous. She was also well known for wearing men's clothing, for which she had a special permit from the police in Paris! She refused to conform to the behavior expected from women at the time, and although it wasn't always easy, she was a happy and successful artist.

You got a permit for those pants?

DRAW ANIMALS LIKE ROSA

The real challenge when drawing animals (and people!) is getting the proportions right. An easy way to start is to draw the very simple shapes and lines that make up an animal's body first, before fleshing out the details. Try copying the circles and lines from the horse outline below, then add color and detail to create a realistic drawing of a horse in motion.

EDMONIA LEWIS

A trailblazing and gifted sculptor, Edmonia Lewis was the first woman of African American and Native American heritage to become internationally famous for her skill in fine arts.

NEOCLASSICAL SCULPTURE

Edmonia created marble sculptures in the neoclassical style, which drew inspiration from ancient Roman and ancient Greek art.

LIVED: July 4, 1844–September 17, 1907

BORN IN: Greenbush, New York (USA)

WORKED IN: Boston, Massachusetts (USA) and Rome (Italy)

> *There is nothing so beautiful as the free forest.*

Edmonia Lewis' parents died before she was nine years old, so she went to live with her aunts. They were Native American craftswomen, and Edmonia started using her Native American name, Wildfire. Many years later she described her childhood as "wild," as she would spend her time wandering through nature, fishing, and swimming. It was a happy time for her, and she enjoyed the freedom of running through the forest.

In 1859, aged 15, Edmonia was sent by her brother Samuel to Oberlin College in Ohio to study art. Oberlin was one of the first colleges to allow women and African Americans to study. In 1864 she moved to Boston, looking for further training in sculpture. There she was turned down by three established sculptors before she was finally taken on by Edward A. Brackett, who made marble busts.

Edmonia held the first solo exhibition of her work in 1864, showing her sculptures of abolitionists (people who campaigned against slavery) and civil war heroes. She made enough money from selling her work to move to Rome, Italy, where she worked for most of her career.

In Rome, she began creating more sculptures in the neoclassical style, for example, showing people dressed in Roman robes, rather than contemporary clothing. Many of her sculptures also had African American and Native American themes and figures, such as her sculpture *The Arrow Maker*, which shows a Native American man teaching his daughter how to make an arrow.

Unlike other marble sculptors, Edmonia did the carving and chiselling of her pieces herself. Other artists would often create wax or clay models, then pay tradespeople to produce the finished marble piece, but Edmonia preferred to do all the work herself to ensure accuracy and originality.

Edmonia was very commercially successful and received two commissions for $50,000 each, an incredible sum worth nearly 1 million dollars in today's money. However, despite her financial success, audience reactions to her work could sometimes be frustrating.

The white people who viewed her work would often assume that her sculptures of women were self-portraits, which Edmonia wished to avoid. She did this by deliberately giving her female figures distinctively European-looking features, but the assumptions people made about her art and the way her pieces were interpreted differently to white male artists was sometimes annoying for Edmonia.

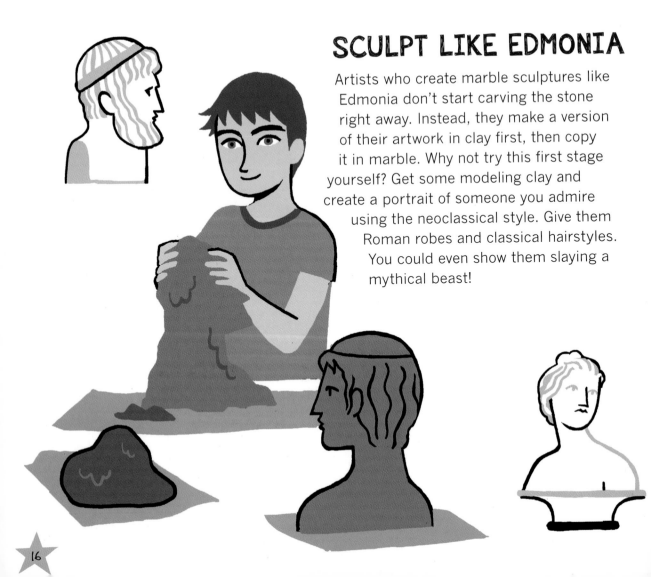

SCULPT LIKE EDMONIA

Artists who create marble sculptures like Edmonia don't start carving the stone right away. Instead, they make a version of their artwork in clay first, then copy it in marble. Why not try this first stage yourself? Get some modeling clay and create a portrait of someone you admire using the neoclassical style. Give them Roman robes and classical hairstyles. You could even show them slaying a mythical beast!

COCO CHANEL

Coco Chanel was a fashion designer and trendsetter who revolutionized clothing for women in the 20th century.

FASHION DESIGN

Coco Chanel created totally new looks and styles of clothing that changed the way people dressed around the world.

LIVED:	August 19, 1883–January 10, 1971
BORN IN:	Saumur (France)
WORKED IN:	Deauville, Biarritz, and Paris (France)

I n August 1883 Gabrielle Chanel was born to a poor laundry woman and a peddler. Her mom died when she was only 12 years old, and her dad sent Gabrielle and her sisters to an orphanage. It was a very strict, hard place to live, but it was there that she learned to sew. Her talent with a needle would end up changing her fortunes.

Gabrielle had to leave the orphanage when she turned 18, so she began working as a seamstress during the daytime, and as a singer during the evenings. She would often sing the popular songs "Ko Ko Ri Ko" and "Qui qu'a vu Coco," and so the soldiers who came to watch gave her the nickname "Coco." Unfortunately, Coco was not a very good singer, and so her career as a performer did not last very long!

She began designing hats instead, and opened a shop in Paris. Her hats did not have huge fancy feathers and bows as was the style at that time, but were simple and chic. When a famous actress wore one of her hats in a play, Coco's business really took off.

As well as hats, Coco started to design
clothes, but her clothes for women were
like nothing people had seen before. She used
lightweight fabrics such as cotton jersey that were
previously only used for men's underwear. She
created simple, easy-to-wear clothes for active
women, without fussy frills and restrictive corsets.

Coco's enjoyment of sailing led her to add striped sailor-style tops to
her collection, as well as trousers for women. She started another trend
when she cut her hair short in a boyish style. She had a totally modern
approach to fashion, and at the time her whole look was revolutionary.

In 1926, Coco designed her iconic "little black dress." It was hailed by the fashion magazine *Vogue* for its elegant simplicity. They called it "the frock that all of the world will wear." And they weren't far wrong! The "little black dress" became a classic piece of design, which is still referenced by fashion designers today.

At the end of her life, Coco lived in the fashionable Hotel Ritz in Paris, France. She died in 1971, aged 87. Even in her last moments, Coco was determined to set the trend. Her last words to her maid were, "You see, this is how you die."

The frock all the world will wear

DESIGN LIKE COCO

Many of the innovations Coco Chanel introduced are still extremely popular today, such as sailor-style striped shirts, bobbed haircuts, and simple black dresses for elegant occasions. Her designs were loved because they were stylish, but comfortable and modern. Try and design a fashion collection of your own in the style of Coco Chanel. Draw a set of clothes using simple, elegant shapes and comfortable fabrics.

FRIDA KAHLO

Frida's colorful and emotionally complex art explored the tragedies that she suffered in her life, as well as her identity as a Mexican woman.

SURREALISM

Frida's very personal artwork does not neatly fit into any categories, but she often used surreal, dream-like images to express her feelings.

LIVED: July 6, 1907–July 13, 1954

BORN IN: Coyoacán (Mexico)

WORKED IN: Cuernavaca, Mexico City (Mexico), and Detroit (USA)

On a summer's day, in a village just outside Mexico City, Frida Kahlo was born. Her mom was Mexican, and her dad was an immigrant from Germany. When she was six years old Frida caught polio, a disease which forced her to stay in bed for nine months. The polio caused one of her legs to be thinner than the other and left her with a limp forever afterward.

During her illness Frida became very close to her dad. He taught her about art, nature, and philosophy and encouraged her to take up sports such as boxing and roller skating to regain her strength, even though at this time these sports were considered only for boys.

Frida was very clever, and at age 18 she was training to be a doctor when tragedy struck again. A bus she was traveling on crashed into a tram, and she was almost killed. She spent many months in the hospital with terrible injuries, and was in pain for the rest of her life. She began to paint while she was recovering, as it was something she could do while lying down.

After two years, Frida was no longer confined to her bed, and she began spending time with her old school friends who were involved in politics. She joined the Mexican Communist Party and met the artist Diego Rivera. She was much younger than he was, but they fell in love and got married.

She began to use Mexican folk art styles in her painting, and wore traditional Mexican clothing. Many of Frida's paintings show self-portraits in which she would emphasize her eyebrows and facial hair to show that she rejected Western ideas about what is "beautiful," and to express her Mexican heritage. Her paintings often showed strange, dream-like scenes which symbolized her feelings, such as one painting that shows her as a deer being hunted with arrows.

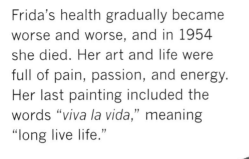

Frida's health gradually became worse and worse, and in 1954 she died. Her art and life were full of pain, passion, and energy. Her last painting included the words *"viva la vida,"* meaning "long live life."

EXPRESS YOURSELF LIKE FRIDA

Frida used surreal images in her paintings to tell the viewer about her emotions and thoughts. She also exaggerated parts of her appearance to make statements about her identity.

Try creating a self-portrait in the same style. Consider what parts of your clothing and appearance would tell the viewer something about who you are and where you are from. Add details or other elements to your picture, such as animals or objects that can represent your personality or feelings. For example, if you think you are usually a brave person, you could add a lion to your picture, or if you have been feeling like the outcast, you could show yourself alongside a black sheep.

YAYOI KUSAMA

Describing herself as "obsessive," and voluntarily living in a mental health hospital for decades, Yayoi's incredible, colorful art has consistently challenged the expectations of the art world.

AVANT-GARDE

Yayoi Kusama has had a very varied career, spanning different media and movements. Her art can be described as "avant-garde," because for much of her career she has been pushing at the boundary of what can be called art.

BORN: March 22, 1929

BORN IN: Matsumoto (Japan)

WORKED IN: Tokyo (Japan) and New York City (USA)

Yayoi was born into a traditional Japanese family in an area surrounded by high mountains. As a little girl she longed to explore what lay beyond. She once wrote a letter to the president of France that said: "Dear Sir, I would like to see your country, France. Please help me." She got a reply from the French Embassy in Japan advising her to study French!

Yayoi loved to make art, but her parents were not supportive of her interest. Her mom would tear her drawings away from her, but Yayoi would not give up and when she ran out of art supplies, she would look around the house for alternative things to make her pictures with.

At age ten, Yayoi began to have hallucinations, which were bright flashes of light with dense patterns of dots. These hallucinations went on to greatly influence her work. A psychiatrist suggested she continue with her art and so, against her mom's wishes, she went to art school in Japan.

I prescribe ART!

Yayoi became very interested in European and American avant-garde art, and in 1957, fed up with Japan, which she felt was too conservative, she moved to the USA. She began creating huge artworks covered in polka dots, from massive 30-ft (9-m)-long canvas paintings of repeated dots, to clothing mannequins that she also covered in dots. She was fascinated by the idea of infinity, and used polka dots to create "infinity rooms."

Polka dots are a way to infinity.

At first Yayoi struggled to make money and often went hungry, but she quickly became an important figure in the New York avant-garde art scene. She created an astonishing range of strange artworks, including installations such as mirror-lined rooms filled with neon balls, huge open air sculptures of pumpkins, and performance art in public spaces.

Yayoi worked incredibly hard, however, she continued to struggle with her mental health. In 1973, she moved back to Japan, and in 1977, she checked herself into a hospital for the mentally ill, where she has been living by choice ever since.

Her creativity and uniqueness have made Yayoi a hugely successful artist. In 2014 she was the most popular artist in the world according to the visitor numbers of her galleries, and a recent retrospective tour of her work attracted over two million visitors. A five-story museum dedicated to Yayoi was opened in Tokyo in 2017.

• CREATE LIKE YAYOI

Yayoi works in many different media (which means the material and method that an artist uses to create a piece of art).

She has created sculptures, installations (such as rooms decorated with mirrors or lights that create sensory experiences), performance art, and huge paintings. One consistent theme throughout her art is polka dots. Create your own piece of artwork with the theme of polka dots: perhaps a painting, or a collage, or polka dots added to an existing object. Can you think of different media that you could use to create a piece of artwork, or new ways to include polka dots?

VIVIENNE WESTWOOD

Creating radical and rebellious clothing designs inspired by music and politics, Vivienne Westwood is a very successful fashion designer and businesswoman.

PUNK FASHION

Vivienne Westwood was largely responsible for creating the "punk" fashion style of ripped fabrics, safety pins, tartan fabrics, and chains.

BORN: April 8, 1941

BORN IN: Tintwistle, Derbyshire (UK)

WORKS IN: London (UK)

From a very young age Vivienne had strong feelings about injustice. In her aunt's shop at age five, she saw an image of Christ on the cross. When she asked her cousin about it, she could not believe what she was told and that people could be so cruel. Vivienne became dedicated to opposing injustice at that point.

Vivienne was born into a working-class family in the north of England, but they moved to London when she was a teen. She briefly studied silversmithing at college, but dropped out, believing a working-class girl could not succeed in art. However, she continued to make and sell her own jewelry while working as a teacher.

Vivienne began to get very involved in fashion when she started a relationship with Malcolm McLaren, an art student who she met through her brother. Malcolm and Vivienne opened a shop in 1971, selling Vivienne's clothing designs. Malcolm was the manager of the punk band, the Sex Pistols, and Vivienne's clothes dressed the band and helped them create their signature look.

Punk was all about a rebellious, counterculture attitude. Punk artists and musicians believed that mainstream culture was restrictive and materialistic. It was a political and cultural movement, and the clothing style reflected its provocative themes. Vivienne created outfits that featured ripped fabrics, accessorized with bicycle chains and dog collars, safety pins, and aggressive slogans. These were the looks that started the iconic punk style of the 1970s and 1980s.

The fame of the Sex Pistols made Vivenne a well-known name in fashion, and in 1981 she held her first catwalk show called "Pirate." It featured unisex clothing designs inspired by pirates with big, billowing sleeves and trousers. Historical costumes became an important inspiration for her design style across her career.

Her later fashion lines also poked fun at establishment and upper-class culture, using elements from 18th and 19th century aristocratic clothing, such as Victorian crinoline skirts. She always wanted her fashion to be fun and outrageous, and she had no time for pompous attitudes! Vivienne's use of historic references in her styles were hugely influential to fashion at the time.

NO TO AUSTERITY

CLIMATE REVOLUTION

FRACKING DESTROYS THE ENVIRONMENT

Throughout Vivienne's career she has often been very outspoken about political issues, campaigning on climate change and on behalf of civil rights groups. In 2015, her catwalk show featured models holding placards with slogans protesting against fracking and austerity. These designs continued to be influential on fashion, in the same way as her punk styles of the 1970s.

She is a hugely successful fashion designer, with many stores selling her collections around the world, as well as being made a Dame of the British Empire by the Queen. Despite her role as an international businesswoman, Vivienne still believes it is better not to be materialistic, advising people to, "Buy less. Choose well. Make it last."

MAKE A STATEMENT LIKE VIVIENNE

Vivienne's clothing designs have always had an element of social or political commentary, since her beginning as a fashion designer in the 1970s punk movement. Think about an issue you really care about—it could be the environment, or perhaps women's equality. Create a fashion collection that makes a statement about your chosen issue. Think about things such as what materials you would use for the clothes—does your choice of fabric say something relating to your message or cause?

ZAHA HADID

A forward-thinking and ambitious architect, Zaha Hadid created unconventional, artistic building designs.

ARCHITECT

Zaha Hadid designed buildings. Like art, architecture has different styles. Some people called Zaha's style "deconstructivist" because of her use of unusual shapes and angles.

LIVED: October 31, 1950–March 31, 2016

BORN IN: Baghdad (Iraq)

WORKED IN: London (UK)

33

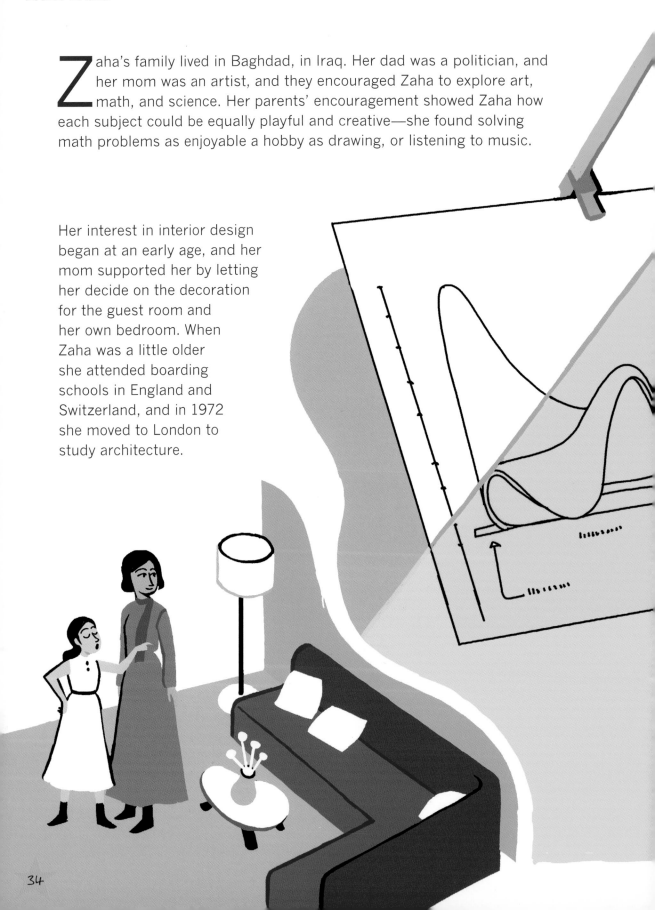

Zaha's family lived in Baghdad, in Iraq. Her dad was a politician, and her mom was an artist, and they encouraged Zaha to explore art, math, and science. Her parents' encouragement showed Zaha how each subject could be equally playful and creative—she found solving math problems as enjoyable a hobby as drawing, or listening to music.

Her interest in interior design began at an early age, and her mom supported her by letting her decide on the decoration for the guest room and her own bedroom. When Zaha was a little older she attended boarding schools in England and Switzerland, and in 1972 she moved to London to study architecture.

Architecture was the perfect combination of her twin loves math and art, and even as a student Zaha immediately rejected conventional architecture styles. Her designs were much more radical, and she insisted on avoiding 90 degree angles in all of her work, instead using unusual diagonals and curves. Her tutor nicknamed her "the inventor of 89 degrees" because of her refusal to use boring right-angled shapes! She later went on to design the famously curved Heydar Aliyer Centre in Azerbaijan.

After graduating, Zaha taught architecture herself at a number of universities, including Harvard in the U.S. and Cambridge in the UK. Then in 1980, she opened her own architectural firm. In the early years, not many of her building designs went on to be constructed, and instead she built up a portfolio of design ideas.

One of Zaha's first designs to actually be constructed was for a small fire station in Germany, although it ended up being used as an exhibition space instead. A very sculptural design with lots of sharp, diagonal angles, it was the start of her career as an internationally successful architect.

In the 1990s and 2000s Zaha gained larger and more prestigious commissions, including the Guangzhou Opera House in China, and the London Aquatics Centre for the 2012 London Olympics, among many others. Her buildings continued to use flowing shapes and avoid straight lines and 90 degree angles. She became nicknamed the "queen of the curve."

Zaha won many prizes and awards for her architecture, including the prestigious Stirling Prize for excellence in architecture in both 2010 and 2011. In 2012 she was made a Dame Commander of the British Empire.

SKETCH IDEAS LIKE ZAHA

Imagine if you could design and build your dream home. What would it look like? When architects like Zaha first start designing a building, they begin by sketching ideas. These first sketches can be as crazy and imaginative as they like, before the later stages of forming a building that can realistically be built! Create a series of sketches for the most over-the-top amazing dream home you can think of. What strange shapes will you use? What bizarre features will your house have? Let your imagination run wild.

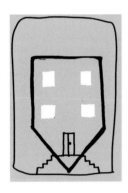

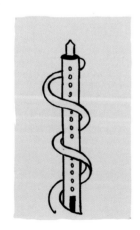

MORE ART AND DESIGN VISIONARIES

The list of visionary women in art and design doesn't stop there! Here are even more pioneering women artists that you should know about, from Renaissance artists of the 17th century to today's rising stars.

JUDITH LEYSTER
LIVED: July 28, 1609–February 10, 1660
BORN IN: Haarlem (Netherlands)
WORKED IN: Netherlands

Judith was the eighth child of a brewer and cloth maker in Haarlem in the Netherlands. It is thought she began painting after her father became bankrupt, and she needed to earn money to support her family. She joined an artists' guild in 1633, which was extremely unusual for women at that time.

She painted a self-portrait in 1633 looking very relaxed and smiling, another break in tradition, as women's self-portraits were much more formal in that era and usually showed serious facial expressions. Her work was well-respected, and she took on several young apprentices.

After Judith died in 1660 she became largely forgotten until 1893, when her signature was found on a painting. Recently, art historians have been restoring her reputation as a pioneering female artist.

HARRIET POWERS

LIVED: October 29, 1837–January 1, 1910
BORN IN: Clarke County, Georgia (USA)
WORKED IN: USA

Talented quilt designer Harriet Powers was born into slavery in Georgia, USA. She learned to sew, probably taught by her mother. She used traditional appliqué techniques, where shapes are cut out of colored fabric and stitched onto a background, to create quilts showing scenes from stories. Her quilts told Bible stories, local legends, and recorded astronomical events.

During her lifetime a newspaper article described Harriet as illiterate, assuming she learned her Bible stories from other people. However, Harriet could read and write, and may well have used her quilts as a teaching tool herself. Only two of her quilts survive, and they are now on display in museums as beautiful and historically important examples of African American folk art.

GEORGIA O'KEEFFE

LIVED: November 15, 1887–March 6, 1986
BORN IN: Sun Prairie, Wisconsin (USA)
WORKED IN: USA

By the age of ten Georgia had already decided she would be an artist and her family arranged for tuition from a local watercolor artist for her and her sister. At art college she was top of her class, and she was very skilled at realistic painting. However, the realist style did not excite her, and she began experimenting with abstract styles.

Georgia painted simplified images of natural things, such as flowers and rocks, as well as abstract and colorful pieces representing her feelings about music. Wherever she traveled, she created artworks that expressed a strong sense of the place and landscape. She became attached to the desert landscape of New Mexico, and she lived and worked there for many years.

BARBARA HEPWORTH

LIVED: January 10, 1903–May 20, 1975

BORN IN: Wakefield (UK)

WORKED IN: UK

When Barbara was a girl, she would look at the shapes of the hills and fields as her family drove through the English countryside. This fascination with the landscape stayed with her throughout her life. She studied art at college, then became a sculptor, creating abstract works of art from wood and stone. She wanted to create art that was calming and beautiful and preferred the method of working directly in the chosen material, rather than the more traditional process of making models from which someone else would produce the work.

Barbara moved from London to the seaside town of St. Ives in Cornwall in 1939 and lived there for the rest of her life. Her love of the landscape continued to inspire her, and some of the large sculptures that she created were designed so that they could be used as a "frame" for the landscape around and behind them. Audiences could look through the center of her pieces to see the world in a different way. She was a very important figure in Modernism, an art movement that used simple, abstract shapes.

LEE MILLER

LIVED: April 23, 1907–July 21, 1977

BORN IN: Poughkeepsie, New York (USA)

WORKED IN: USA, France, and UK

American fashion model, photographer, war correspondent, and artist Lee Miller lived an extraordinarily varied life. At age 19, she was about to step in front of a car in New York, but the publisher of *Vogue* magazine spotted the danger and pulled her to safety. This was how she was "discovered" as a model, and she appeared on the cover of *Vogue* in 1927.

In 1929, she traveled to Paris to study with the surrealist photographer Man Ray. She became friends with famous artists, including Pablo Picasso, and created many photographic artworks. She moved to London, and after the outbreak of World War II in 1939, she became a photojournalist for *Vogue* magazine. One of her stories documented the Blitz, the German campaign of air raids on London and other UK cities from September 1940 to May 1941.

After the war Lee traveled to mainland Europe and photographed images of Nazi concentration camps for *LIFE* magazine. Due to the horrific things she saw, she suffered from a period of poor mental health, and gave up most of her photographic work, becoming a gourmet cook.

EMILY KAME KNGWARREYE

LIVED: 1910–September 3, 1996

BORN IN: Utopia (Australia)

WORKED IN: Australia

E mily was nearly 80 years old before she began to paint. She was an Indigenous Australian woman from the Anmatyerre community, and the area where she was born was settled by white cattle farmers when she was around ten years old. She spent much of her life working on cattle farms, until the land where she was born was returned to Indigenous Australian people in 1976. In 1977 she learned batik-making, a method for printing designs onto silk fabric. The patterns she used were inspired by traditional body markings, as well as being symbolic of important plants that grow in the Australian desert. She moved from batik to painting with acrylic paints on canvas in the 1980s, and created many incredible, colorful artworks that became internationally popular and sold for hundreds of thousands of dollars.

LOUISE BOURGEOIS

LIVED: December 25, 1911–May 31, 2010

BORN IN: Paris (France)

WORKED IN: USA

L ouise was named after her father, Louis, who had wanted a son. Family life was difficult when Louise was a child, because her father had an explosive temper and was unfaithful to her mother. As a teenager she cared for her frail mother, who died when Louise was 21.

Louise met her husband Robert in 1938, and emigrated from France to the USA where she studied art. She used her art to express her difficult feelings from her childhood. She created many different kinds of art, including huge metal sculptures of spiders, strange installations, and drawings of body parts.

BASTARDILLA
BORN: ?
BORN IN: Colombia
WORKS IN: Colombia

No one knows exactly who Bastardilla is. Like the British graffiti artist Banksy, she keeps her identity a carefully guarded secret. What is known is that she is a very talented and unique street artist from Colombia, whose artworks cover powerful topics such as violence against women, police violence, and poverty. She has gathered an international following, and has created large pieces not only in her home country of Colombia but in cities around the world, including Mexico and Italy. Although her art features serious and often dark topics, her murals are brightly colored, and she even uses glitter to make the artworks sparkle at night.

KARA WALKER
BORN: November 26, 1969
BORN IN: Stockton, California (USA)
WORKS IN: USA

Art has been a passion for Kara since she can remember. One of Kara's earliest memories is sitting on her father's lap, aged two-and-a-half, watching him draw, and thinking "I want to do that too." Born in California where she lived until she was 13, she then moved to Georgia, where she found that racism in society was much more out in the open. Her experiences in Georgia inform her art, which explores race and the history of slavery in the southern states of the USA.

Her most well-known artworks include large cut-paper silhouettes showing exaggerated caricatures of figures from the era of slavery. At the age of 27 she became the second youngest recipient of the John D. and Catherine T. MacArthur Foundation's "genius" grant, which is a prize for extraordinary individuals working in any field.

COUNTLESS OTHERS...

The women included in this book are just a very few of the amazingly talented, visionary artists and designers who have made art, and continue to make art around the world right now.

GET INVOLVED IN ART AND DESIGN!

It doesn't take much to get started on the path to being an artist. Just pick up a pencil and paper, a piece of clay, some fabric or a camera, and give it a try! That's it! Kara Walker said, "There's no diploma in the world that declares you an artist ... You can declare yourself an artist and then figure out how to be one." But if you need a bit of inspiration, here are some other ideas for how to learn more and get involved in different types of art.

GO TO GALLERIES AND MUSEUMS

It sounds obvious, but one of the best ways to get started on creating your own art is to look at the work of other artists. Visiting galleries and museums can give you great ideas for different topics and styles to try out yourself. Lots of people teach themselves to make great art by copying some of their favorite pieces by famous artists; this is why you'll often see people in galleries sketching.

Museums and galleries often run special events and workshops for kids, too. Look online to find a gallery near you, and find out what interactive events and activities they are putting on.

FIND AN ART CLUB, OR START ONE YOURSELF

Look for an after school art club you can join, and if there isn't one, start one yourself! You can try out different art styles and techniques each week. Books from the library can give you project ideas, or look for tutorials on YouTube to learn drawing techniques. At the end of the semester, you could put on an exhibition of your artworks for your family and friends to enjoy.

ENTER A YOUNG PERSON'S ART COMPETITION

Perhaps you're the kind of person whose competitive spirit will help get your creative juices flowing. If so, there are tons of art competitions for children and young people on various different subjects. Search online to find a competition on a subject or style that particularly interests you.

GLOSSARY

Abolitionist A person who campaigned to have slavery made illegal.

Abstract A style of art that does not try to show things realistically, but focuses on color, shape, and ideas.

Austerity Policies put in place by the government to reduce spending, which involve cutting public services or lowering payments for people who can't work.

Avant-garde An art movement that uses new, experimental methods and ideas.

Bust A model of a person's head and neck.

Caricature A cartoon-like image that exaggerates someone's features.

Chiaroscuro A style of painting (and photography) that uses strong areas of light and shade.

Deconstructivist A style of architecture that has very unconventional shapes, and can give the appearance of the building being broken up or fragmented.

Establishment The people and organizations that hold the most power within a country.

Fracking A process through which fossil fuels (coal, oil, gas) are extracted from the ground.

Illiterate Unable to read and write.

Indigenous people The first people to settle a land.

Materialistic Overly concerned with money and expensive objects, rather than more important issues.

Modernism A broad art movement in Western society at the end of the 19th and early 20th centuries that often used simple abstract shapes.

Native American People from one of the many groups who were living in North and South America before Europeans arrived.

Naturalistic A style of painting that aims to show things close to how they look in real life, as opposed to abstract styles.

Nazi A member of the right-wing political party, led by Adolf Hitler, which was in power in Germany from 1933 to 1945.

Neoclassical An art style that uses designs from ancient Greek and Roman art.

Peddler Someone who travels from place to place in order to sell things.

Pigment A colored powder that is mixed with liquid to make paint.

Psychiatrist A doctor who studies and treats mental illnesses.

Retrospective An exhibition showing an artist's body of work from over a long period of time.

Seamstress A woman whose job is sewing and making clothes.

Slavery The system by which people are owned by other people as slaves.

Still life A painting or drawing of inanimate objects, such as fruit or flowers.

Surrealism An art movement that shows strange, dream-like scenes, inspired by the unconscious mind.

FURTHER INFORMATION

WEBSITES

Check out the Tate galleries' kids' website for lots of ideas for fun and crafty activities that could be done at home or in an art club setting. **kids.tate.org.uk/create**

Art charity National Open Art runs a competition for young people in the UK and Ireland up to 14 years of age. **www.nationalopenart.org/children.php**

Find out about American artist Aminah Brenda Lynn Robinson and create your own art. **aminahsworld.org**

For an informative and entertaining introduction to art and art history using computer-based tools to encourage exploration and creativity, visit the following website from the National Gallery of Art: **https://www.nga.gov/education/kids.html**

Explore artists, art movements, fashion, design, museums, and culture at: **https://www.google.com/culturalinstitute/beta/**

BOOKS

The Story of Paintings by Mick Manning and Brita Granström (Franklin Watts, 2017)

13 Women Artists Children Should Know by Bettina Schümann (Prestel, 2017)

Good Night Stories for Rebel Girls by Elena Favilli and Francesca Cavallo (Particular Books, 2017)

Fantastically Great Women Who Changed the World by Kate Pankhurst (Bloomsbury, 2016)

INDEX

First edition for the United States, its territories and dependencies, the Philippine Republic, and Canada published in 2018 by Barron's Educational Series, Inc.

Text © copyright 2018 by Georgia Amson-Bradshaw
Illustrated by Rita Petruccioli
Volume © copyright 2018 by Hodder and Stoughton
First published in Great Britain in 2018 by Wayland,
an imprint of Hachette Children's Group,
part of Hodder & Stoughton

All inquiries should be addressed to:
Barron's Educational Series, Inc.
250 Wireless Boulevard
Hauppauge, NY 11788
www.barronseduc.com

Library of Congress Control No: 2018939577

ISBN: 978-1-4380-1217-9

Date of Manufacture: May 2018
Manufactured by: WKT, Shenzhen, China

Printed in China
9 8 7 6 5 4 3 2 1